BEAUTY

ASHES

GRACIE SHAVELL

BEAUTY
ASHES

Printed in the United States of America
First Printing
ISBN 978-1-955148-65-8 (pbk.)
A2Z Books Publishing
Lithonia, GA 30058
www.A2ZBooksPublishing.net
Manufactured in the United States of America
A2Z Books Publishing has allowed this work to remain exactly as the author intended, verbatim.

References:
NIV Bible-New International Version
The Power of God's Name Tony Evans pgs 211-214

DEDICATION PAGE

To my mother, Tootsie, who gave me life. To my Godmother, my Black Diamond, who gave my heart a home when I needed it most. To my father, Boutte, who gave me the best life he could with what he had. Thank you. I am who I am today because of your lives, love and sacrifices. God be praised!

CONTENTS

CHAPTER 1: EL NEHKUMAH

"The God Who Comforts All"

March 1996 —a month and year that will forever go down in history as the worst season of my life. On that cool winter morning, I woke up needing to use the restroom. I tried to wake up my mom, but I could not wake her. At that moment, I didn't know it, but my mom had suffered a seizure that caused her demise. I spent what felt like hours standing at the window, crying out for help. I was not allowed to go outside alone, so I opened my parents' bedroom window in hopes that someone, anyone, would hear me. My dad wasn't far away. He was across the road in the woods at my great uncle Al's house. My parents' bedroom window ran perpendicular to his driveway. When standing at the window did not work, I went to stand on the porch. I screamed as loud as I could until help came. Those were some of the most vulnerable moments of my four-year-old life. As I stood on the porch and at the window, screaming for help, the feelings of hopelessness began to overtake me like never before. I was afraid. I didn't know the magnitude of what was going on, but I knew it wasn't good. My life was about to change completely.

I remember feeling so helpless, afraid and alone. All I could think was "Someone! ANYONE! Please help me!" That feeling of helplessness followed me for years as if my inner child had become a prisoner inside of me and I instantly had to mature faster than most children my age. I never knew how much of a prisoner I was within myself until the older me began to go back to that day to face the horror of it head-on. It was a day that marked and shaped my life in more ways than one. It was a day that played a part in me being the woman I am today.

My father finally heard my cry for help. Upon arriving home, he started to attempt CPR. He began to call various people in my family. One of my mother's aunts was one of the first in the family to arrive at our home. They attempted everything they could to bring her back but nothing they attempted was successful. By nightfall, EMS had arrived on the scene. By that time, cars were lined up for miles and miles. Family from everywhere filled our two-bedroom mobile home while others waited outside. I vividly remember comforting my older cousins who were in my bedroom awaiting the final verdict of my mother's status. In attempts to comfort them, I went up to them in an attempt to comfort them. I remember hugging them and telling them that "Everything is going to be okay." It was at that moment that four-year-old me acted as a caregiver and the caregiving hasn't ended.

I remember my mother's funeral. We were in the old sanctuary at Pine Grove M.B. Church. There were so many people there. I remember my dad picking me up and allowing me to kiss my mother on the forehead. After her funeral, there was a gap in my memory where I could not remember anything until the next person died in my family. I could remember deaths as clear as day, but I couldn't remember being a Girl Scout before my mom died and I couldn't remember other life events. Many years later, I would discover that memory loss was a normal part of grief, and that I would often remember the traumatic things over the good things. The reality of my mother's death did not sink in until years later. I would be so envious of my friends who had the gift of celebrating their mothers on Mother's Day, while I didn't have anyone to celebrate. As I grew older, I began to develop anger towards God. To be quite frank, I didn't want to have much to do with God for several years as a teenager. Now, I know what you're thinking: "You were just a rebellious teenager like all the others." I'd say that there's some truth to that, but at the core of it all, my rebellion was fueled by my anger, bitterness, and resentment towards the Lord. I couldn't understand why such a loving God would take my mother away from me. I wanted Him to hurt as much as I hurt.

My mother's death was not the only death that affected my life. Before I was born, my maternal grandmother and a great-uncle died. After my mother died, I lost one of my mother's sisters that same year. The next January, I lost an uncle on my dad's side. After his death, I lost my maternal great-grandfather and my maternal grandfather. Some years after that, I lost a great-aunt and another great-uncle. It was as if death itself had a chokehold on my family and it would not let go. To top off all the losses, one of my favorite first cousins died on my 16th birthday. It was the worst birthday I'd ever had and one I'd hoped for years that I'd forget.

Death had become my new normal and it felt like I had no way out. As life began to change for me, the older I became, I battled with how a loving God would allow me to go through so much at such an early age. The trauma of losing my mother affected me deeply until I was 30 years old. With all of that, I would often find myself asking, "How could I surrender my entire life to someone whom I had been conditioned not to trust? Why would this God that I am supposed to serve take so many people that I love—and who I didn't get to know— away from me?"

In reality, God was the only true-life raft I had left. It took me 26 years to realize that, but I know that now more than ever. When I felt the most alone, God was the only one who truly knew how to comfort me. Although I didn't understand the concept of His love and comfort, I would soon find out as the years went by. God is truly the God who comforts all.

CHAPTER 2: EL ROI

"The God Who Sees"

Grief and trauma opened me up to great darkness, demonic curiosity and sexual sin through masturbation. I was introduced to the demonic realm through scary movies around the age of eight and was later introduced to masturbation closer to my teenage years. I found a source of peace in self-pleasure because it was a form of comfort for me to release all of my cares and worries. I didn't realize that it was sinful until years later, but even then, I was already living the way I was going to live, so I just continued to do it until I replaced self-pleasure with the peace of God.

I always watched scary movies, both suspenseful and demonic. When I was nine, I had a dream that my Great Aunt Sadie died, and I was with her when she died in the dream. The next morning, I woke up and my dad informed me that she had died in the night. From that place and experience, I was even more curious about many things. I began to dive deeper and deeper into the occult. Although I never played with "Ouija boards" or palm readings, I did develop an obscene curiosity about demons. I also played into astrology through reading my horoscope (a taboo topic, but it is very much a part of the occult). These things and many others opened me up to the enemy in a way that is hard to put into words. They separated me from God because it caused me to give myself over to the kingdom of darkness and my sin became my identity.

At the age of nine, I asked God to be my Lord and Savior. Two days before my 10th birthday, I was baptized. I spent many years after that in what I call a "wrestle with God." I knew there was something different and special about me, but I didn't know what it was. It took me to go through the fire at an early age to learn that there was so much more than what meets the eye. Around the age of 15, I hit my "breaking point." I was angry with God, my family, my mom, myself, etc. Over the years, the weight of grief, emotional turmoil and many unanswered questions had built up. But about two years before I hit my breaking point, my Godmother, whom I called my "Black Diamond," came into my life. She became the home my heart desperately needed. Through her life and legacy, I "inherited" six siblings, all of whom are older than me. This provided me with a sense of family which I had longed for. My Black Diamond was there for me through all my winning moments and even the hard ones. She was my second chance at having a mother and although she was not my biological mother, her love for me was no different. She was a gift that was sent to me exactly when I needed her the most. I would end up losing her years later and the hole in my heart would become greater after having lost a second mother, but I had a better understanding and deeper revelation of God being there for me through her presence in my life. Her playing a role she didn't have to play made me realize that God saw me & He knew what/who I needed most. Although losing her in the flesh was one of the hardest experiences I've endured in a long time, I knew that she had found the peace and rest she needed the most.

Although the dynamics have changed with my "inherited siblings" since her death, there has been one who has been near and dear to my heart. As I continue to seek the Lord for what our relationship looks like without my Black Diamond, the language of our relationship has changed from "God-brother" to "brother". We have experienced some "growing pains" over the last few years, but there's no other sibling that I would rather fight for & "choose violence" with (inside joke. Lol) than him. No matter where life takes us, I will always have his back and will be right there with him & for him. He knows. During that time when I was in a "wrestle with God," I vividly remember going up before the congregation of my mother's church and asking for prayer because I felt so broken. I exclaimed to the church, with tears in my eyes that "I don't feel like anyone loves me." The pain of my past and present haunted me like a monster or demon in a scary movie. I felt as if my life had no purpose at all. I couldn't see past the pain and my fears. I couldn't see past the anger, bitterness and the loneliness that I felt. It was in that season, as I look back now, that God revealed Himself to me as ABBA —my Father.

What do we know about Fathers? They protect and lead us. They correct our wrongs; they love us when we are at our lowest and they speak life over us when we're surrounded by darkness. In that painful season of my life, God revealed His love for me when He kept me from taking my own life. I had gotten so low and depressed that I didn't want to live anymore. I became suicidal. I used to take scissors and cut my wrist often. Occasionally, I would take a dull knife and attempt to do the same thing. I feared killing myself because I grew up being told that, "you would go to hell if you killed yourself." So, killing myself was not an option. With that ideology before me, I knew that I didn't want to go to hell, but I didn't want to live anymore, regardless. The pain and agony I felt from so much loss, trauma and torment became my kryptonite. I began to die spiritually, so much so that I figured it would be easier to die physically than to continue to fight. It was at my point of breaking, that the God that saved me spiritually at the age of 9, came to save me physically and emotionally at the age of 15.

During one of our Sunday School classes, my cousin who was my teacher at the time, went around the room and began to prophesy to us. When she got to me, she told me that I would be a missionary. On the inside, I scoffed and said to myself, "She has no idea what she is talking about. How could God use me when I am so sinful? How could He use me after all the things I've done?" Although I felt so inadequate and unqualified because of my sin, I was right where God needed me to be; broken because He was preparing to put me back together piece by piece. Peace by peace.

My cousin's obedience to God by speaking prophetically into my life was the life raft that I needed. I had the ammo that I needed to fight the spirit of suicide, and the hope deferred that I felt started to slowly but surely leave me. Over the course of the next two and half years, the wrestling continued but it was a battle between my flesh and my spirit. I hit rock bottom only to be built anew from that point on. I fought to learn more about God and who He was in my life.

On December 31, 2009, I gave my life back to God. I decided to leave my life of active sin and to live for Jesus for the rest of my life. Unbeknownst to me, that was only the beginning of my journey with the Lord. I had no idea that the next twelve and a half years would bring so many highs and lows, but that it would point me to the place I'm in now. A few months later, I was preparing to graduate from high school. I knew that I could not do it without God, so I started putting in the work to get closer to Him. At the time, I was used to curse like a sailor. Johnny Depp had nothing on me, and I mean that. My language did not align with the lifestyle I wanted to live, and I knew that had to change. I began to ask God to take what I called "that cursing demon" away from me. I asked Him to transform my heart in the process. He answered my request and so much more. Everything that I had gone through was divinely preparing me for the journey that God was preparing for me. It was a journey I never imagined being on, but one that I am so eternally grateful for. God is truly the God who sees, and He specializes in turning our ashes into something beautiful.

CHAPTER 3: "YAHWEH"

"The God Who Keeps His Word"

Numbers 23:19, "God is not a human, that he should lie, not a human being that he should change his mind. Does he speak then not act? Does He promise and not fulfill?"

After graduating from high school, I began my journey at Northeast Mississippi Community College. One of my main prayers before attending Northeast was that God would surround me with godly friendships and that those friendships would help me grow closer to Him. Not only that, but I also prayed that those friendships would help me get to where I was supposed to be in life. Upon moving to campus at Northeast, I was introduced to the BSU — Baptist Student Union. Once I became connected at the BSU, I started making friends, and also took the steps toward becoming a summer missionary. The verse referenced above was about to come to fruition in my life in ways that left me forever changed. God had spoken a word to me four years prior that saved my life and now that word was about to give birth to one of the sweetest and greatest journeys of my life at the time.

After getting connected into the BSU, I started attending their luncheons and student-led events. From there, I started participating in evangelism at the apartments close to campus. When I began the journey of evangelism, I had no idea how to share the Gospel or my faith in general. I shadowed those who were more seasoned in evangelism until I became comfortable doing so. At some point, I was "put on the spot" and I had to go with what I had in my metaphorical "tool belt". This journey continued over the course of my first semester. All of the door-to-door assignments prepared me for what would turn out to be the mission trip of all mission trips.

On January 14, 2011, I went on my very first mission trip out of the state. This mission trip was to evangelize on Bourbon Street in New Orleans, LA. Our mission field that weekend included evangelizing to people who, essentially, came to "get drunk and have a good time." New Orleans, also known as the "Big Easy", is known for its "fishbowl and hand grenade" drinks. The "Cat's Meow" was the one club/bar we could see as we walked down St. Peter Street leaving the main French Quarter strip. When we saw the club, we knew we were on Bourbon and that we were close to the church, Vieux Carré, which was our headquarters that weekend. That weekend of ministry transformed my perspective of people, the church, sin and brokenness in more ways than one.

Keep in mind that I was still VERY NEW to sharing the Gospel, my faith and being comfortable with sharing it with other people. I went from sharing with those in apartment complexes in small town Booneville, MS to trying to witness to drunk folks on Bourbon in an atmosphere designed to "chew us up and spit us out." I did it and although I had many fears that weekend, I was "all in" because I wanted those who were hurting, broke and dying to know about a Savior who could save, heal, redeem, and set free; just as He did for me. I gained so much insight from the realities of the real world. To be honest, because of where I grew up, I thought that all Black people were saved. So, seeing Black people on Bourbon Street who were not saved broke my heart. It also made me even more aware of the brokenness in my family.

Bourbon Street Ministry stirred up a deeper burden in me, to reach the lost with the Gospel of Jesus. It helped me to love sinners in a way that I never knew I needed to. It caused me to look at the world around me with new eyes; eyes that only God can give. These eyes helped me to see the broken just as God sees them. I was a different person after that weekend.

What I didn't mention earlier is that when we arrived in New Orleans, it was about 9 p.m. We were parked on the other side of Dauphine Street unloading our van. I suddenly heard someone yelling and cursing someone. All I could think was, "Someone call my dad and tell him I'm not going to make it home because they're going to kill me." I look back and laugh now, but in all honesty, in the moment, it wasn't as funny as it is now. I often look back at that time and laugh because four and a half years later, I would move to New Orleans and live there for six years. It was humbling that God would use someone like me to lead others to His Kingdom. I felt unworthy, but the Lord knew exactly what He was doing. I had no idea that all those moments I encountered in ministry would bring me to the place and season I am in now.

Matthew 28:18-20 (NIV) says, "Then Jesus came to them and said, All authority in heaven and on Earth has been given to me. Therefore, go and make disciples of all nations, baptizing them in the name of the Father, and of the Son, and of the Holy Spirit, and teaching them to obey everything I have commanded you. And surely, I am with you, always, to the very end of the age." Jesus not only commissioned the disciples, but he gave them a mandate. It wasn't "if you or when you go make disciples", He said "GO and MAKE disciples"; no questions asked. That charge and mandate didn't die with the first disciples. That charge and mandate still lives and is still expected of us today. After my first weekend in NOLA, I knew I wanted to devote the rest of my life to telling people about Jesus; not just as a missionary, but in another capacity as well. Between the Great Commission and my own transformation experience, I desperately wanted to extend the same hope that had been extended to me to others.

Although New Orleans was my first mission trip outside of the state, I felt like I needed to do missions at home before traveling the world. Before I would go on my first short-term mission trip as a summer missionary, I took a group of college students to my hometown of Starkville, MS. We did door to door evangelism in a neighboring town that I grew up in called Crawford, MS. No one accepted Jesus Christ as their Lord and Savior that weekend, but we were able to plant seeds of prayer and hope. I continued to go on my NOLA mission trips during MLK weekend, but I later branched out into the missions arena.

Summer of 2012, I became a BSU Summer Missionary. BSU Summer Missions takes place every summer from May to August or the end of July. Summer Missions are for those who feel called to give up their summer to share the Gospel with those they're assigned to. Anyone who is interested in summer missions would apply for either North American Missions (missions that take place within the United States) or International Missions. I became a summer missionary for three out of the five years I was in college. In summer of 2012, I was a SM at Mission Arlington in Arlington, TX. Later that year, I went on my first international mission trip to East Asia. For the safety of my brothers and sisters in the faith, I will not share the location of where we were. During the summer of 2013, I was a SM in Sand Springs,

OK. Due to the nature of that ministry, I am keeping the name undisclosed. Later that year, I returned to the same place where I went on international missions the year prior. It was not in my plans to return, but I met someone through my BSU who was interested in going and she mentioned to me that her mother was not going to allow her to go alone. It was in that moment that I knew that the Lord was preparing to send me back. Although I wanted to be home with family during that season, I knew that I was supposed to go; not just for the new friend that I made, but God allowed me to see how the seeds that we had sown the year before had begun to produce Godly fruits. I was also able to embrace a new sister in Christ from the year before who was experiencing great rejection from her family because of her newfound faith.

In 2015, I was a SM at Baptist Friendship House in New Orleans. I completed my assignment one month before I moved back there for seminary. All these trips continued to mold and shape my faith in God. During my short-term international mission trip, we were not allowed to use words like "God, Jesus, bible, church, missionary, Gospel, prayer, Holy Spirit", etc. because of the religious restrictions in that area. We had to speak in code whenever we shared the Gospel with those we were called to serve because we didn't know if we were being followed or watched at any given point. When I came back to the states, I reflected on that time and if I can be completely honest, I was angry. I was angry with the Church of America because we were so pacified and entitled when it came to our faith. We often place unrealistic demands on people or personal gain, and we overcomplicate religion in the ways that we do when it should ALWAYS be about a relationship with the Father, Son and Holy Spirit. We have churches on every corner and yet we take advantage of our freedoms because we think that we "don't need the church and all that

Jesus stuff is unnecessary". We were beginning to become a generation who was more concerned with "being spiritual" than we were with being committed to a relationship with God and it angered me.

For the longest time, I did not want to go to church in America. I just wanted to be with my new brothers and sisters in the faith. I wanted to help them grow and mature in the faith because they were hungry and thirsty after the things of God more than they were concerned with the "Sunday's best" fashion shows and turning the house of God into a "den of thieves" by making it everything but about the Lord. Still, this new revelation made me want to be more like Christ in everything that I aspired to do. 1 Timothy 4:12 says, *"Don't let anyone look down on you because you are young, but set an example for the believers in speech, in conduct, in love, in faith and in purity."* This had not only become my life verse, but my heart's song and I did not allow myself to be short-stopped at anything else.

As my Bourbon Street Ministry trips began to transform my faith, so did all the other trips. Serving others taught me how to shift my prayer life through intercession. It challenged me to be more intentional in prayer and taught me the importance of praying specifically for others and even myself. It increased my love for people and instilled in me a devotion to want to live on mission for the rest of my life. II Corinthians 5:17 says, *"Therefore if anyone is in Christ, he is a new creation; the old has gone, the new has come."* The more I began to submit to the Lord to "Go and make disciples," the more the old Gracie continued to fall off and the more I stepped into newer depths in my relationship with the Lord. Although I was being sent on a mission to share the Gospel with others, the Lord was doing a greater and deeper work in me.

My surrender to the Lord on December 31, 2009, was only the beginning of my transformation into being a "new creation in Christ." The more I surrendered to the Lord, the more my life began to reflect that surrender. My language began to change. My heart's posture began to change. My surrender came without reservation because I felt like I had nothing to lose. Although I had an awareness of the cost, the cost could not compare to the greater things that God was preparing to do in me. I was "all in, heart abandoned, arms wide open and ready for whatever" when it came to my relationship with the Lord. The more I dove deeper into my relationship with the Lord, the more I began to see His character unfold in many facets of my life.

In the midst of all the mission trips I was going on, I made two moves. One in 2013 to Cleveland, MS, to attend Delta State University, and again in 2015 to New Orleans to attend seminary at New Orleans Baptist Theological Seminary. When I reflect on my time at Northeast, I rejoice in the Sovereignty of God over my life. When I first started at Northeast, I wanted desperately to be a nurse. After having lost my mother at such a young age, I wanted to be for others what I wish someone was for me when I needed them most.

My hardest obstacle in that journey was conquering Anatomy and Physiology, also known as A&P. I could not conquer it, which opened the door to hopelessness and feelings of defeat. I wanted nothing more than to be a nurse and could not see myself being anything else. I remembered walking down the road one night talking to God and I said, "Lord, I know that you have not brought me this far to leave me. Please show me what I am supposed to do and where I am supposed to go." I left it in His hands that night. A few days later, I met with the school's guidance counselor and let her know what my passions were and asked her to help me choose a major that would not set me back academically, but one where I could fulfill my passions and one where all my credits would count towards.

During that meeting, she spoke to me about Social Work. My first words to her were "I don't want to take nobody's kids away from them." She began to educate me on the perks of social work and what that would look like moving forward. She informed me that Delta State had one of the most prestigious Social Work programs in Mississippi. I began to pray through and consider the possibility. A short while later, a recruiter from DSU came to NE to provide program information and help sign students up at DSU. God had begun to orchestrate everything as it should be, and one thing led to another. My next step was DSU. I was both excited and nervous, but I knew I was making the right decision and right move for my life.

CHAPTER 4: JEHOVAH GOELEKH

"The God Who Redeems"

In August of 2013, I started my journey at Delta State. The transition was very challenging for me. It was my first big move away from my friends. The funny part is that I was not homesick for my family in Starkville as much as I was homesick for being away from Booneville. Before graduating from Northeast, I started visiting the Wesley Foundation, which is the Methodist student organization. I needed a break from the BSU world for many reasons, so the Wesley was where I began to attend. While I was there, I met a couple who were dating at the time. We ended up transitioning to DSU at the same time and this helped greatly with my transition because we had something in common; but I still missed my core friendships at Northeast. Although I missed my best friends, having familiar faces with me helped me more than words could express. Another friend of mine from Northeast also transferred to DSU around the same time, and we met on the Quad during Meet-and-Greet Week. God knew what I needed more than I knew during that season.

While being at DSU, I began to plug in to the Wesley Foundation more than I did the BSU. I attended BSU on occasion so that I could still participate in mission trips, but the Wesley was where I spent most of my time. I only had two summers left to be a summer missionary, so I had to stay connected as much as I could. Although the Wesley did not offer the same type of mission field as the BSU, I was fortunate to partake in international student ministry on camps, which is where my heart was ultimately.

Our International Student Ministry entailed us serving students who represented over 90 different nations. During that season, I fell in love with many countries and cultures represented. These countries included, but were not limited to the following: Egypt, Iran, Iraq, South Africa, Brazil, Mexico, France, Australia, Ireland, etc. On Thursday nights, we would host "International Nights" where we gave the students the opportunity to cook some of their family's national dishes while sharing the story of their origin. It was a perfect depiction of Heaven on Earth to me. We were able to disciple some of the students that came through the ministry, and we had many of them profess Christ as Lord and Savior during my time there. We would also show our support for them by attending their games if they played sports or if they had some sort of academic program on campus, we would attend as much as we could. Both the International Nights and supporting them throughout the school year gave us the opportunity to be an example of Christ in our service and support throughout the school year.

Getting to serve these students was one of the sweetest seasons of ministry for me since leaving Northeast. Not only was I able to see a depiction of what Heaven will look like, but I was also able to love on others the way Christ calls us all to do; "love your neighbor as yourself." Each student and nation represented was my neighbor and I was honored to be able to serve them in such a way. Growing up in a small town like I did, having exposure to another country and other nations was a gift to me, and I was humbled to know that God would entrust me with the assignments that He did trust me with.

Between serving in East Asia short-term and being a part of the international student ministry, I began to see the Great Commission in a different light. Going and serving nations had a new meaning for me and I wanted to go deeper. That new season of ministry also highlighted, all the more, that I didn't always have to "go," but that the nations were at my doorstep, and they needed it just as much as those who I would have to travel to via plane.

Another blessing of being a part of the Wesley was gaining an amazing group of sisters in the faith through our ladies' Bible Study Group. Our bible study group challenged me in my faith in more ways than one. It also provided me with the tools that I needed to continue to grow and mature in my personal relationship with God. For example, I grew up being taught about the importance of memorizing Scripture, but I was never taught how to memorize Scripture. Our amazing leader, "Kay Kay" (is what I will call her), gave us different tools through her personal growth in the Lord, as well as through things that she would learn in her leadership training. The spiritual discipline of scripture memorization ushered me into a deeper dimension of praying God's word through understanding and application.

We were later assigned accountability partners. During our season of having accountability partners, we were to meet once a week with one another. During that week of meeting, we were to talk about our week, recite our memory verse to one another, repent of anything that we felt we needed to repent of to one another as a means of accountability, and then we were to close in prayer for one another. Having this blueprint and means of serving one another was a blessing for me and would help me greatly in the seasons to come. I grew in my love for the Word of God as well as in my love for sisterhood. I was blessed with many gifts, and their sisterhood was one of them.

In addition to the continuation of my mission's journey to increase my spiritual growth and maturity, I was enjoying my journey in Social Work. As I discussed the journey to the decision about social work in chapter three, I had no idea what I wanted to do with the degree and what the road ahead would look like, but I was prepared to embark on whatever I needed to embark on. I fell in love with the educational side of social work and began to realize the importance of advocacy and being a voice for others who may have had their voice taken from them. The more I embarked on the journey and learned the different avenues of social work, the more I fell in love with the idea of whatever God had in store for me next.

During my last semester at Delta State, I completed my residency at a nursing rehab facility. I helped with case management as well as referrals. I did a lot of office work and I was also able to visit the residents and help the director of activities to perform activities with the patients. It was one of the most amazing yet challenging experiences as a senior Social Work student. The challenging parts were when the patients would die and sometimes the families were not ready. Or when the patients would be having an exhausting day, and they became increasingly agitated. I fell in love with working with geriatric patients and sought to do so post-graduation, but the Lord had other plans. Although many things in my world did not make sense at the time, God would eventually bring all of the pieces of my puzzle together. Not only would things later come together, but my experiences would begin to make sense.

With graduation in sight, I began to pray about what I was supposed to do for my next season. With ministry in mind Social Work being my career path, I began to seek the Lord for His will for my life in the next season. I wanted to stay in the Delta to pursue my MSW (Master of Social Work) degree to be closer to my friends, but I also felt a call to seminary. I began to pray a bold, but specific prayer. You see, with social work, you must have A's and Bs in your core classes to finish your masters in a year. This program track is called "Advanced Standing." So far, I had kept the requirements for the MSW Advanced Standing Program. So, my prayer was, "Lord, if I do not receive a C in any of my classes, I am staying here in Mississippi so I can be close to my friends and family; and I will go to Mississippi Valley State for my MSW. BUT, if I get a C, I will go to seminary IF that is what I am supposed to do." At the end of that semester, I landed a "C," the ONLY "C" in one of my core classes. It made no sense for me to have a "C" in it. So, seminary it was.

As I reflect on all that had transpired in the years prior during my time at Northeast, and even during my time at DSU, I realize that God is not only the redeemer of time, but that He does not waste anything. God was preparing to use all my heartaches, disappointments and pain to allow me to minister to those who needed to hear what I had to say. In addition, He did not allow any of my school credits to go to waste at Northeast and I did not have to be in school longer than anticipated. Although I did not have the language that I have now back then, I knew that God had a greater plan and story prepared for me.

CHAPTER 5: JEHOVAH RAPHA

"The God Who Heals"

As God prepared my heart for seminary, I had no idea what I was getting myself into. All I knew was that He said "GO" and I said "YES." The path that I envisioned for myself looked nothing like the path that I was on, but I knew that it would all come together as it should. I was ecstatic for the journey ahead, but I was nervous at the same time. Either way, I was about to be living in my favorite city and it would be the first time I ever lived out of state long term. Leaving my family was not easy, but New Orleans turned out to be one of the best 'yes' I had ever given the Lord and to this day, I have no regrets.

My journey to New Orleans reminded me a lot of Abraham's journey with the Lord. In Genesis 12, the Lord called Abram, later renamed to Abraham, to leave his native country to go to a land He had prepared for him. Genesis 12:1 says, *The Lord had said to Abram, "Go from your country, your people, and your father's household to the land I will show you."* Later in Genesis 17, the Lord made a covenant with Abram and told him that He will "make him a father of many nations," which we later know as the 12 tribes of Israel. HUGE deal, right? RIGHT!

Much like Abram, I had no idea what I was getting myself into, but I knew the voice of God was leading me and, in His sovereignty, He was preparing me for something bigger than myself but nothing ever bigger than Him. My "faith move," much like Abraham's, came with many challenges, tears, what-ifs, stumbling moments, anger, intercession, me leaning on my own understanding, me trying to make things happen my way, etc. But in every season, in every way, the Lord's love and mercy restored me in moments I needed restoration and His grace ushered me into one of the greatest, most significant seasons of my life and I could not be more grateful, humbled, thankful, and blessed.

God showed me the many sides of His character during my time in New Orleans. He began with Him being my Jehovah-Jireh, the God who provides. When I moved to New Orleans, I had $250 to my name. I had no idea how I was going to pay for seminary, how I would provide for myself, or how I would live in general. Suddenly, the "spiritual high" of giving God my yes began to wear off and reality set in. More than that, this season exposed the fear in my life and heart on a greater scale and it began to reveal the deep bondage that I was still in. But God revealed it to not only "heal it," but to deliver me and to usher me into a deeper relationship with Him.

This move was not only radical in nature, but it was also the defining moment of all the times I had to step out in faith and trust God. Most times, those who grew up in poverty like I did become fixated on the financial side of faith, but my faith had to go deeper than money. I not only had to continue to trust God with my path, but I had to now learn how to trust Him with the healing of my heart and soul from wounds that I had no idea I had.

Before we get to the things about my wounds, I want to unpack what it looked like for me to be in the "somewhat foreign land" called New Orleans. Mind you, I knew the French Quarter like the back of my hand, but I had only visited the seminary when going to the LifeWay Bookstore that was on campus at the time and when I participated in the MissionLab program during the summer of 2014. MissionLab is the mission's program that is connected to the seminary known as the New Orleans Baptist Theological Seminary. I lived there for about two and a half months prior to moving there because I was a summer missionary there in 2015, but that was only a small glimpse. All the other times, I left to go back to Mississippi, but this time, New Orleans was HOME! I could not put into words how nervously excited I was to live in another state, but the homesickness of missing my friends kicked in heavily during the first semester. But as God did in my transition from Northeast to Delta State, the Lord provided me a tribe to find safety, refuge and comfort in, which made the transition somewhat easier.

When I first started seminary, I was a counseling major. I wanted to go into Christian Counseling, somewhat because of my experiences in my residency during my time at Delta State, but again, I still wanted to be in the medical field and counseling would allow that for me to a certain extent. God allowed me to pursue this degree for an entire year until He, yet again, would wreck my plans and call me to something else. This time, He had a keen sense of humor to get my attention.

Prior to my move to New Orleans, I had a neighbor "up the road" from my dad's house who had begun to invest in my life. She and her Sunday School class adopted me and when I would go to visit, I would go out to lunch with them and share what the Lord had been doing in my life. My next visit with Mrs. JG would be a very mild "Damascus Road" experience, but one that grabbed my attention nonetheless. I was due to meet Mrs. JG at her home to go visit another family that she and her Sunday School Class had adopted. She wanted me to meet them and offer prayer for them as she felt as if I could relate more to what they were going through. As I was preparing to leave the house to meet her, my 2007 Pontiac G6 would not start. I did not understand why because I had no prior issues with it to my knowledge. My dad was not home, so I had no help with getting anyone to jump me off. I called Mrs. JG to pick me up and she did. As we were driving to meet with this family, I heard the Lord say to me VERY AUDIBLY, "I want you to teach my children." I literally looked at Mrs. JG and asked, "Did you hear that?" It was as if the voice was coming from the radio. I later stated, "I think the Lord wants me to change my major." She asked to what and I said, "I'm not sure. He just told me to teach His children." I went back to the seminary and changed my major to Christian Education that week. Talk about an interesting change of events and plans. But yet again, all my credits from my year of being a counseling student transferred over to my next degree program and I did not have to stay in school longer than anticipated. God. Wastes. NOTHING.

Now, some of you may be asking what happened to my car. Well, I got home later that afternoon and my dad was there. He LITERALLY only lifted my hood, and my car cranked. Wild, right? God was very strategic in this encounter to get my attention because He knew that driving myself there would be distracting and He needed me physically still and in a posture of listening and receiving what He was about to tell me. But also, it is because He knew I would feel like someone placed about 200 lbs.. worth of cinder blocks on my chest when I heard His voice, and I did not need to wreck (Lol).

So, I changed my major and thus began my journey as a Christian Education major; but it was not the only journey I was about to embark on. You see, the four-year-old Gracie who had endured so much trauma, heartache and pain was still at the forefront of now 24-year-old Gracie and there were things that the Lord needed to address. As I went through my journey, I began to realize all the more that God brought me to the seminary to connect me to those who would help me begin my journey to emotional and spiritual freedom. My education and degree, in that season, was an added bonus. Although I had no idea what I was getting myself into, I knew that there were things that needed to be dealt with. In spite of the fear I felt, I knew it was time.

During my time in New Orleans, the Lord introduced me to inner healing and deliverance ministry. Many refer to it as "Sozo" ministry. Sozo, in Greek, means "salvation, healing, deliverance and wholeness." Sozo ministry focuses on the healing of the mind, body, soul and spirit. I hadn't realized that I needed all of these things until the Lord began to surround me with people who not only spoke life into me, but who would shed light into my behaviors and fears. The Lord took me through extensive Sozo's over the course of years. During that time, the Lord highlighted the deep-rooted seeds of rejection, unforgiveness, bitterness, anger, insecurity, FEAR (a MAJOR stronghold in my life), the poverty mindset, shame, guilt, etc. It took many years to dismantle a lot of those strongholds in my life, but with a lot of sacrifice, tears and being surrounded by the right prayer warriors, I was able to gain breakthrough in many of those areas.

Now, some of you might be wondering what a stronghold is. A stronghold is anything that's present in your life that keeps you from being able to move forward. For example, fear was a stronghold in my life that kept me from being able to live freely. Because of all the traumatic experiences I had gone through, I had a crippling fear that something bad would happen and I would die. I would sometimes not allow myself to enjoy life or experiences with people because I would have the mindset that I was going to die, so it didn't matter what I did. The stronghold of guilt and shame kept me from accepting God's forgiveness of me and in return, I wasn't able to forgive myself. These Sozo encounters were the beginning stages for a life-long transformational journey that would change my life forever. There were things that I'd have to revisit from time to time, but the Lord fortified my healing in such a way that freed me forever.

Not only did I participate in Sozo ministry in different seasons, but I also had Christian counselors who came alongside me to assist me in my freedom. The thing about being made up of mind, body, soul and spirit is that when one of those areas is under attack, it usually affects other parts of us as well. For me, I needed healing in my emotions because of all the things I had been through. I would often struggle in my relationships because if anything happened that would resemble any traumatic event I had lived through in the past, I would struggle emotionally. I battled with separation anxiety. I would develop soul ties with people out of fear of them leaving me —in life, in death and sometimes both at the same time. I would hold people so tightly that I would create emotional soul ties with them. I specifically did this with men who made me feel beautiful or gave me time and attention because I never received it from my father. My father never told me I was beautiful and a lot of times we barely said "I love you" (that part has changed over the years).

Soul ties are strong emotional and physical connections made between two or more people. You can have sexual soul ties through having multiple partners. If you have had more than one sexual partner before marriage, if you have not had those soul ties broken, you carry them into your marriage. You can have emotional soul ties by having an unhealthy codependent relationship with a person or multiple people. Some soul ties are healthy. For example, when you get married, you create a soul tie, a bond, with your spouse that should remain within the confines of your marriage and "marriage bed."

Although I had never had sex before, I had an emotional soul tie for seven years (at the time of working through these soul ties) because I thought that God would "heal and change him," and that he would be my husband. I couldn't see my life being with anyone else. He was the first man who made me feel loved and the first to give me the time and attention that he gave me. He would shower me with gifts during my birthday and at other times as well. The downfall is that he was bound to sexual sin and had not been putting in the work to actively be transformed. Because of that, and many other reasons, the Lord did not allow him to be my husband. I had to let go of him emotionally and relationally (in our friendship) because I made a vow in my emotions and heart that he would be my husband. This emotional soul tie would have kept me from opening myself to be loved by anyone else because of the layers of bondage that came with it; had I not dealt with it from the root."

Those soul ties and other deep-rooted seeds of darkness positioned me before God for a miracle and my miracle was the healing that I would receive over time. God knew that New Orleans would be a season of greater depth in Him and He had to remove me from what was familiar to me to bring forth that healing, but to also launch me into deeper destiny. Step by step, the Lord held my hand and led the way for me. Through those encounters, God loving on me through His people and Him loving on me Himself led me to the next season of life. My current season still required much heart check and soul work, but with the Lord's leading and help, I was able to break through and break forth.

CHAPTER 6: JEHOVAH SHALOM

"The God Who brings Peace".

My season in New Orleans was slowly coming to an end. Although it felt like no end was in sight and I had to fight the discontentment of the season I was in, God was preparing to use all of my experiences in my childhood and my current season to prepare me to minister to people who needed what I had. It was 2021 and I had been working in the NOBTS Cafeteria for almost three years. I was becoming stir crazy and to be frank, angry and discontent. In 2019, I vividly remember telling the Lord—just one month post-grad school graduation —about all of my degrees and accomplishments. As I was griping and complaining about still working in the cafeteria, the Lord almost audibly said to me, "I'm not concerned with how many degrees you have. I am concerned about the posture of your heart." In my own words, I had "several seats."

At the time, I didn't realize the effects that anger and bitterness had on me. I was angry with God for the season I was in. I was bitter about the workplace treatment I was receiving at that time. I was jealous that other people I graduated with were moving on with their lives and I felt stuck. All the while, the enemy was having a field day with my heart and mind and I had given him full permission by coming into agreement with his lies, the bitterness, anger, resentment and control.

Although I was not behaving as a child of God in my heart, the Lord was still moving, working and orchestrating things on my behalf.

In 2020, during all the racial tensions in our nation, the Lord began to work on my heart and give me a desire to make a difference in the lives of our law enforcement officers. I began to have conversations with various officers who served with the NOPD about their needs and how we could bridge the gap between law enforcement and our communities. During one of my conversations with someone who had come through the cafeteria, they began to talk to me about becoming a chaplain. A police chaplain. Chaplaincy was never on my radar, but I began to entertain the idea of chaplaincy and started to pray more in depth about what I was supposed to do with such. Then 2021 came around and everything began to fall apart—as it fell into place.

In January of 2021, an associate of mine at the seminary informed me that the Clinical Pastoral Education director at Baton Rouge General emailed the seminary about their CPE program they offered at the hospital for those who wanted to go into chaplaincy. The CPE program was a year-long residency that taught you how to do marketplace ministry through chaplaincy. Marketplace ministry entails bringing ministry into the secular world. The medical field has a great need for marketplace ministers who have a heart to love and serve others from every tribe, tongue, nation and religious background.

After receiving the information, I began to work on my resumé. After completing the application and my resumé, I was later told that I had been accepted into the program and that I would begin in September of 2021. I was ecstatic and overjoyed to begin the journey of walking out my purpose to bigger and better things. I got the news in March of 2021. In May of that year, I took a pay cut by quitting my job in the cafeteria and going to work in the coffee shop until I moved to Baton Rouge. It was the craziest thing I had done in a while, but I knew that my summer would have been miserable and exhausting had I not quit. The scrutiny was not worth the money and I learned that I had decided to step out in faith and trust God to provide. And He did.

Fast forward to August of 2021. The month that changed my life in more ways than one. Earlier in 2021, I decided to go through *Restoring the Foundations* (RTF), which is an inner healing and deliverance ministry. RTF consisted of five days of working through generational curses and bondage along with inviting God to come in to perform deeper healing and deliverance in my life. There were several things that were keeping me bound and I desperately needed freedom. The groundwork that I had done in the years prior to RTF prepared me to go deeper in my healing. The biggest area of focus was getting set free from the bondage I took on when my mother died. It was as if the four-year-old Gracie was still trapped on the inside of me and I couldn't move forward. We went back to the day my mother died (for me, it was another layer that I had to work through even after the prior healing) and I finally felt the freedom I had been searching for. I was finally free from the grief after having carried that baggage for almost 26 years. After I received my healing, the inevitable happened.

During my RTF trip, I received a text message stating that my Black Diamond was in the hospital after becoming ill. While I was receiving the deeper work I needed to be set free from the grief of losing my mother, my second mom was in the hospital fighting for her life. My heart felt so torn. All I wanted to do was hear her voice and hold her hand. I wanted to tell her that it would be okay and that God was going to heal her. I wanted that, but God had other plans.

I turned 30 on 8/21/2021. I didn't even think I'd live to see 25 and yet I was not only turning 30, but I had tapped into a deeper freedom that I spent the majority of my life waiting for. Ten days later, I received a text message that my Black Diamond had gone to be with the Lord. I was crushed. I felt wounded all over again, but in a different way. It felt as if someone took the wound that I was just healed from and they pierced a knife through it and opened it all over again. I lost another mom: The one who came to my graduations and didn't miss a beat. The one who supported me in all of my ministry endeavors. The one I would always call when I was somewhere new and she'd say, "Gracie, you don't let any grass grow under your feet, do you?" The one I came home to for holidays and who always made me laugh with her funny sayings. My heart was broken all over again. While I was still trying to maintain my healing and deliverance that took 26 years for me to receive, I was now grieving the one I had never seen my life without. The one who would be the mother present to help me get ready for my future wedding and the grandmother to my future children. I felt robbed of my time with her. I felt robbed of what could have been for our future relationship now that I was made new and felt more whole.

That season of my life was one of the hardest I had been through in a long time. Not only did I lose my second mother, but I was an evacuee two days before her passing, as Hurricane Ida was about to sweep through South Louisiana and bring utter devastation to the surrounding areas. I was in the midst of preparing to move to Baton Rouge and nothing was ready. It felt like so much was coming at me and I couldn't keep up.

The timeline of that season went like this: August 21st - I turned 30 years old. August 29th, Hurricane Ida made landfall as a Category 5 hurricane and was a Category 4 by the time it reached New Orleans.

August 31st, my Black Diamond went to meet Jesus. In the midst of all of this, I wasn't packed for my move that was supposed to take place in two weeks. I was couch and bed surfing as an evacuee and to top it all off, I had no clue where I was going to live because the weekend I was supposed to go apartment hunting (again) was the weekend Ida hit. The week of the funeral, I drove from Starkville, Mississippi, to Baton Rouge to find an apartment then drove back to Starkville that same day. That's a 5-hour drive each way. I was in the car a total of about 13 to 14 hours and I did it all alone. Three days later, we buried my Black Diamond. I drove back to New Orleans the next day. Two days later, I had to commute back and forth between New Orleans and Baton Rouge for three days that week because my residency had started, but my apartment wasn't ready for me to move into just yet. That was about a 3-hour drive round trip; 1.5 hours each way (and without traffic, it was less than that).

When I moved into my apartment that weekend, I had to make one more trip to NOLA to get all of my things. I had no furniture, so I was sleeping on an air mattress that a friend of mine had given me. By the time I FINALLY settled down, I felt as if I was having an out-of-body experience. To be completely transparent, it took me until April 2022 to feel like a person again. The intensity of my grief caused me to have severe migraines to the point where I would have to sit in the dark when I came home from work. I honestly didn't know if I was "coming or going" at that point. I would cry intensely some days because the weight of missing her would weigh on me. I would have encounters with the people I met and served in the hospital that would remind me of my Black Diamond and it would cause me to weep when I got home.

I felt so alone in my grief. Here I was in a new city and a new season and I was having to learn how to navigate my grief alongside everything that life was throwing at me. I didn't have the support I desired from family who had the shared experience with me, but the faithfulness of Abba Father was so evident in my life. He placed trustworthy people in my life to help me heal and who would be present and listen when I truly needed someone to hear my heart. Although they were not the people I wanted to be there, they were the ones I needed. I am eternally grateful for the tribe I had during that season and if you are reading this book, you know who you are. THANK YOU!

Fast forward to September 2022; I completed my residency and received my certificates for completing four units of Clinical Pastoral Education. I was now ready to pursue my career as a chaplain but I had no idea where I'd go or what I'd do. It took six months for me to find a job, but through a series of connections and prayer, the Lord opened the door for me to work in hospice. I was honestly TERRIFIED to work in hospice because my car was 17 years old at the time and I was petrified that it would break down while I was driving. But a year and three months —almost to the day of me starting my work in hospice—the Lord opened the door for me to buy a BRAND NEW CAR (a testimony and answer to prayer in and of itself!). God took my FEARS and transformed them into FAITH. I only broke down once during that time and it was because my alternator went out on me. It wasn't much longer after that breakdown that I received what I had been praying for. And God went ABOVE AND BEYOND for me. I couldn't have been more thankful and grateful.

The moral of my story and journey is this: God wastes NOTHING. God REDEEMS time, experiences and moments —those that tried to, and some were meant to take me out. In the midst of so much uncertainty, in the midst of so many storms I've endured in my 33 years of life so far, God has been my peace. In moments of my life when I expected death, God gave me life. Where there was so much chaos, He was my peace. All of my experiences with death, loss and grief prepared me for my journey in hospice. I am still working in hospice to this day and I would not trade this journey for anything in the world. Now, I get to be for others—in their moments of both anticipated and actual grief, what I wished someone would have been for four-year-old Gracie. And for 30-year-old Gracie. God redeems time and He CAN/WILL restore the years that the locusts destroyed when we place our hope, faith and lives in Him. I am grateful for the God who knows, who sees, who heals, who redeems, who restores and who saves. It is an honor to serve him with my whole life and heart.

CHAPTER 7: YESHUA "THE LORD MY SALVATION"

A s I was writing this book, I felt as if the Lord had placed it on my heart to extend the invitation to Salvation. Scripture says that *"All have sinned and fall short of the glory of God."* (Romans 3:23). Scripture also says that *"The wages of sin is death but the gift of God is eternal life in Christ Jesus our Lord"* (Romans 6:23). What does this mean? It means that because we were born into sin, we desperately needed a Savior, a Redeemer, to come in and pay the price for our sins. In Old Testament Scripture, in order to make atonement (payment) for sin, God would give specific instructions on what needed to be sacrificed so that our sins could be paid for. The first instance of a sacrifice made for the atonement of sin was in Genesis when Adam and Eve sinned in the Garden of Eden. When they sinned, God killed an animal to clothe them because they became aware that they were naked after eating from the Tree of the Knowledge of Good and Evil. Genesis 3:21 says, *"The Lord God made garments of skin for Adam and his wife and clothed them."* It was from that point on that man had to make atonement for sin through sacrifice.

It was the sin of Adam and Eve, the first of mankind's creation, that brought sin and destruction into the world. Their sin caused them to be kicked out of the Garden where they once communed with God, thus separating us from God. Until Jesus came on the scene. God saw that the sin was becoming greater and greater in the world, so He sent his one and only Son, Jesus Christ to make atonement (to become the ultimate "Lamb sacrifice") once and for all. John 3:16 says, *"for God so loved the world that He GAVE his only begotten son, that whosever believes in Him should not perish, but have eternal life through Jesus Christ."*

What does this mean for us as God's creation and His children? We have the opportunity to now have a relationship with God without the restrictions we once had before Jesus came. We get to come into the presence of God and have a relationship with Him like Adam and Eve once did before they sinned. Because Jesus died for our sins, we no longer have to pay the price for our sins when we accept Him as our Lord and Savior. WHAT A PRICELESS GIFT WE HAVE BEEN GIVEN!!

This chapter is specifically for those who have not accepted Jesus as their Lord and Savior, as well as those who have accepted Him as Lord and Savior, but who have lived for the world the majority of their lives. Baptism alone does not save us. Confession alone does not mean that we are in a relationship with Jesus. We have to confess, believe and actively work out our salvation with fear and trembling through obedience to Christ (Philippians 2:12). Many people believe that they are saved and have a relationship with God just because they were baptized when they were young and they accepted Jesus into their life, but to be called a "Child of God", we must have a relationship with Him and we must not live as the world lives. We have to "be in the world" and not "of the world".

For the unbeliever who has never accepted Jesus Christ as their Lord and Savior, pray this prayer with me: "Lord Jesus, I come to you today as a sinner in need of a Savior. I have spent my entire life searching for something and someone to fill the voids in my life, not knowing that person is You and it has always been You. I invite you into my life and my heart to be my Lord and Savior. I invite you into my life to heal me, redeem me from sin and to set me free. I invite you into my life to heal and deliver me from the chains of sin that lead to death, darkness and destruction. I acknowledge that salvation is a lifestyle and I commit myself to not just being saved, but living saved. Come into my life, transform my world and set me free from the Kingdom of darkness, but to live out my salvation through a relationship with Jesus Christ. I choose this day to live my life for you until you call me Home into your eternal rest. Send me trustworthy believers who will disciple me and bring me into the family of God that you have ordained for me in this season. I pray this all in your Son, Christ Jesus' name, AMEN!"

For those who have strayed away from God and who need to be restored back into the body of Christ, pray this prayer with me: Father God, I repent for straying away from my relationship with you and away from the teachings of your Word. I repent for squandering my Kingdom inheritance as a Child of God and for trading my inheritance for the things of this world. I repent for choosing to please the desires of my flesh over living a life governed by the Holy Spirit of God. I repent for thinking that a life led by you is not as worthwhile as living a life I chose for myself. I choose, this day, to live for you again. I choose, this day, to trust you with my life and future again. I choose, this day, to lay aside the desires of my flesh that lead to death and to live a life governed by the Holy Spirit which leads to life. Forgive me for my sins and cleanse me of all unrighteousness. I choose this day to give you my life, again, once and for all. In your Son, Jesus Christ's name, AMEN.

If you prayed a prayer for salvation, WELCOME INTO THE FAMILY OF GOD!!! If you prayed a prayer of repentance for being like the prodigal son, WELCOME HOME!! Here are a few things you need to know: God can instantly transform your life in some seasons, but other seasons may take more time for you to be set free from your past way of living. Have grace for yourself and receive the grace that God has for you. If you fall, KEEP GETTING BACK UP!! This is a lifestyle, not a marathon. It is normal for you to grieve your sin. It is normal for you to cry out to God to change you to be more like His image. This is what He desires for you: To come to Him for transformation and for you to not feel that you have to do it on your own. The saying that goes "come as you are" has nothing to do with clothing or your outer appearance, but more so with your heart's posture of humility and surrender. I am excited for you and for all that God has in store for your life! Welcome to LIFE!

BONUS CHAPTER

"What I wish they would have told me"

I felt inspired to write a bonus chapter about what I wish people had told me early on in my journey with the Lord. My hope for this chapter is that it will encourage and empower you all in your faith journey with the Lord. Know that the words I write are from a real place and my personal experiences. There have been many others who can also attest to these words and if you are one of them, keep persevering. Your labor is not in vain.

"What I wish they would have told me"

I wish they would have told me that this Christian walk would not be "a cake walk or a leisurely walk in the park". I wish they would have told me how much the enemy would use the people closest to me to try to break me down piece by piece; peace by peace I wish they would have told me how much the enemy would use the people closest to me to try to break me down piece by piece; peace by peace. I wish they would have told me that many in my family would not be supportive of me, as I wished they would be. I wish they would have told me that much of my rejection and betrayal would come from family because I was no longer that broken little girl who could be easily manipulated and controlled. I wish they would have told me that my family and closest friends would hold my past against me, as if it were a badge of honor to make themselves feel less convicted by the Holy Spirit at work in my life. I wish they would have told me that they wouldn't respect my position in ministry because I am a woman.

I wish they would have told me that the people I once walked closely with and respected would not respect me for my Christian values and position; although they profess to be Christians themselves. I wish they would have told me that being my authentic self would be a threat to those who refuse to deal with their insecurities, selfishness, sins and shame/regret, just as I once had to do. I wish they would have told me that becoming a better version of me would mean that I'd lose people that I never imagined losing because they loved me broken and bitter instead of healed and whole.

I wish they would have stressed how costly the anointing is and that being a generational curse breaker would mean that I'd be so isolated from everyone else in seasons of pruning. I wish they would have told me that I couldn't take everyone with me into my winning seasons because some of the people that I wanted to hold close would end up sabotaging me. I wish they would have told me that it's okay to let go of people even when it's hard. I wish they would have told me all this and so much more.

Some of you may be asking, "Why are you telling me, Gracie?" I'm glad you asked. I'm telling you because I want you to know how strong and courageous you are. It takes a different and deeper measure of strength to endure the things I listed above and keep going. I'm telling you because I want you to know that you are not alone. There are many seasoned believers and maturing ones who have felt the sting of maturity and growth in the Lord. Yet, in the midst of the weightiness, they established their true foundation on the Solid Rock, who is Jesus Christ and they did not waver.

I am telling you because I want you to keep going and not to become weary. Scripture says in Galatians 6:9-10, "Let us not become weary in doing good, for at the proper time we will reap a harvest if we do not give up. Therefore, as we have the opportunity, let us do good to all people, especially to those who belong to the family of believers". Therefore, I am telling you so that you don't become sidetracked, disgruntled, discouraged, easily angered/offended, and defeated. You serve a Living God and a RISEN Savior Who loves you dearly, and there is nothing in their eyes that goes unnoticed. Your job is to stay focused and stay the course. Everything and every one else will fall into place as it should.

Lastly, I am telling you because I want you to feel empowered and encouraged that you are in one of the greatest seasons of your life. Whether you are in the midst of a battle or whether you are on a mountaintop, our Abba Father is there with you and He will never leave nor forsake you. Your season of warfare is an indication that breakthrough is on the way and your mountaintop is an indication that you've overcome the battle that kept you in the wilderness and now YOU HAVE WON!! Both seasons are important in your Christian faith. Don't lose heart! Don't allow anything or anyone to cause to you relive a season due to anger and bitterness being stored up in your heart! Keep clean hands and a pure heart at all times. Your greatest adversary is satan and your greatest defender is your Abba Father; the Creator of the Heavens and the Earth! Jesus has already overcome the world, beloved, and it's a fixed fight.

Jesus has already overcome the world, beloved.

Be encouraged, brothers and sisters in the faith. Our King is coming back for us soon and very soon.

With love,
Gracie Shavell

ABOUT THE AUTHOR

Gracie Shavell is a native of Starkville, Mississippi, and currently resides in Baton Rouge, Louisiana, which she considers her home for this season of life. From a young age, Gracie sensed that she was unique, though she never quite knew why. She has a deep love and passion for the arts, which she expresses through singing and worship from the stage at her local church, sharing her adoration for the Lord.

Professionally, Gracie is a Hospice Chaplain. She provides emotional and spiritual support to patients and their loved ones, assists with funeral planning when needed, and performs services when her patients are not members of a local church or specifically request her to do so. To find respite from the emotional weight of her work, Gracie enjoys traveling to different states and countries, as well as taking quick weekend getaways to New Orleans—her personal version of a "staycation." She is also the founder of "By His Grace D-Lites," where she combines her artistic talent to create a variety of flavored pound cakes.

While her background has primarily been in missions and ministry, Gracie is now exploring other avenues where her creativity and mission-minded spirit intersect. She holds an Associate of Arts degree from Northeast Mississippi Community College, a Bachelor of Arts in Social Work from Delta State University, and a Master of Arts in Christian Education from the New Orleans Baptist Theological Seminary.

Outside of work and travel, Gracie loves making memories with friends and family and enjoys cooking as a way to bring people together—whether for friends or visiting family. She looks forward to days when her home is filled with loved ones, pouring out love and blessings to those who need it most. As a single woman hopeful for marriage and motherhood, she dedicates her time to serving the Lord and others in the best way she can, while also investing in her personal growth and self-care. If she could offer one piece of advice, it would be to "Do it afraid," because while fear is just a feeling, faith is a mindset and a posture of the heart before the Lord.

Contact info:
FB: Gracie Shavell
Email: grobins334@gmail.com

Interested in Writing/Publishing a Book? Visit
A2Zbookspublishing.net